Tropomorphoses
Myths from the Evening of Humanity

also by Yulalona Lopez
Night Wolves
Coyote Redux

Tropomorphoses
Myths from the Evening of Humanity

Yulalona Lopez

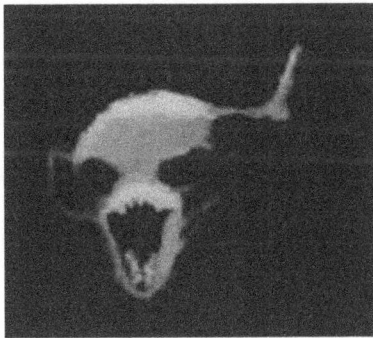

Calliope Press 2007

This Calliope Press Edition of Tropomorphoses is
Published by Mozart & Reason Wolfe

Prepared and produced by Calliope Press,
   Boston
Designed by Rian Ecological Redesigns,
   Cortez

Please address all correspondence for the author,
M&RW, Ltd., Calliope Press, Palouse Poets
Collective, or Riain Ecological Design to:
   editor@3musesbooks.com
   lopez@3musesbooks.com

Second Printing

ISBN 0-911385-11-8

Contents

Angels (make-up on paper)

Respectfully dedicated to the friends who inspired me:
M.E.R.W., C.J.H., H.M.M., and M.L.C.

Ars est celare artem.

Animus fert dicere formas mutatas in nova corpora.
  Ovidii Metamorphosen
(My mind inclines to speak of forms changed into new bodies).

Introduction

The poems presented here are an extension to the Metamorphoses, the Latin masterpiece by Publius Ovidius Naso, written in the year 8 A.D., that recounts a series of transformations of humans into animal, plant, and mineral forms. Ovid's stories range from remote mythic times to the founding of Rome. Poets have long recounted the stories of human beings being changed into other beings. These myths are repeated over and over in many cultures and many times. These myths show us how literally pigheaded humans can be and what just punishments or rewards are meted out; coincidentally, the myths may have helped us to understand other beings by becoming them.

For every myth told, however, there are many not told, and these shadow myths track our cultures, appearing only in fragments and allusions. One important difference between these and Ovidian stories is that these myths describe the conversion of mineral, plant and animal forms into human beings; and this conversion results in different kinds of challenges, that result from openings and expansions instead of closings and contractions. I have assembled a few of them here. These new beings are not gods, so much as the offspring of life beleaguered by human interference, symptoms of the changed rhythms of the earth. Their shapes are new; their names new and unknown. Perhaps these new myths can go further in forcing us to evaluate our attitudes and behavior toward nature and other beings. Perhaps they will be ignored.

These stories take place in the present and relate the turning of other beings into human form (in fact, the title, *Tropomorphoses*, means turning forms). The transformations happen everywhere around the world. A tree in India, a dolphin in Japan, a water lily in Brazil, a wolf in Canada, a bear in the United States, a giant fungus in Germany, a deer in Africa, an eagle in the Philippines, a stone in Australia, and a meteor in the South Pacific. The faces presented are unknown, but demanding of recognition and consideration. Perhaps they can generate at least a small part of the same passion and awe as their predecessors have for centuries. Perhaps not. You decide.

As Heroditus questioned of the Olympians, how can we know if they are eternal or powerful or whether this is their final form? Perhaps we cannot know. Instead, the mystery of living beings presents a Pandora's box of ideas and possibilities of other ways of living. The day of humanity has ended, and the evening begins.

1. Chandi and Rudra Stand

A woman hugs an ash tree
wishing the loggers would go away
would come to their senses and give up.
Time taken from collecting dung for fuel—
Chandi wonders how long she can wait
and not work for food.
She presses into the bark tighter
wishing the tree would come alive and defend itself.

Light
and pressure.
Pressure from the light and
food from the light—sweetness.
Pressure from where light ends
pressure from the wind.
The absence of light
The cycle of light and not.
The coming of water and not
The pulling together into the self
of light and water
The cycle of expanding
Anchored in the dense source
reaching to the light source
spread so far between
taking so much.
Waves of feeling converted to pressure,
feelings, bad feelings, threats

She thinks: "Why can't you stand up
to those who would cut you down?
Why isn't your strength enough?
You can resist wind and fire and almost
time. Why not this, too?
Why not be the guardian of the forest
that men would cut all at once and go?"
She felt a weak thumping against her chest.

Tracheid cells stiffened and hardened into bone,
while vessels became carriers for gum that became
blood. Parenchyma cells became nerves and muscles. The
bark softened. The twigs and branches contracted
into hairs. The roots contracted into hairs. The
pain of contracting, of losing the spread for
catching the light and water, made him
moan above her head.

Changes accelerated. The very air acquired more
sharpness. The ground dragged at him. Light
narrowed to a point. His organs concentrated. He
felt cut off, withdrawn into heartwood. He was
aware of other beings nearby.

She gasped and released him, stepping back.
He leaned to her, swinging his arms in front
astonished that they could move so much
without breaking. Then he turned, fell and lay still.
She knelt before him, speechless and wild-eyed,
touching his shoulder. He thinking: "I am fallen
and will decay now." She thinking: "Miraculous!
The holes of the roots are at his feet. His skin still
rough and grooved, but softening."

Stability, centrality, what had he traded and for what?
To lie still, shrunken and limp, no roots, no leaves,
no twigs, no fungus, unable to collect light
beyond a barely noticeable tickle? Had ever one of his
kind changed so beyond knowledge or return?
Back to the seed? Unheard of.

She shouted at the other women and loggers to help
carry him. Not having seen the change, three of them
carried a naked stranger to a place at the edge.
They looked into green unfocused eyes—the cycle of light
blinked on and off.   He felt pressure on his back and limbs,
stronger than wind or light. He saw pale beings moving
through the standing people. Thought: "Oh, living source
of light, if you have power, let me stand and think again."

10

The answer: "Who are you? How did this happen? Are you
not a tree?"   He understood, without knowing how. "Are you
              not also a tree?" he asked. She moved her lips. He thought:
              "I sweeten light and blend it with earth. I hold the elements
              together. Yet I am held together by my people—separated now."

"You must be a God. Are you Rudra, come to hunt and slay
men? You must help us against those who would destroy
the forest." Her eyes widened.
                              He asked, shocked at the odd
                    wind from within him: "Forest? Standing people?
                    Why would we all be destroyed by them? With what
                          replaced? Can you not all hold light?"
She implored: "They collect
you for tokens that can be used for food and shelter
for things they need in the future. They care nothing for what
is not like them; traditions have been discarded.
You will be used and discarded and not replaced."

She covered him with a cloth and helped him to sit—he
amazed that he did not break. "You must help us. Help us
to stop the cutting the destruction of the forest. It cannot be
replaced."
                    He lay back, thinking at closer to the old pace, on
              the value of his being and that of others: "Who should live,
              who should not. Should difference thrive, and if all became
                    the same, would not difference arise again through
                    the sameness? Once there was naught, you know, but
                          standing peoples and their friends."

Over days, she watched him waste away. A crude hut was built
over them; food was brought, and she ate but he would not.
People, even some loggers, came to see. But, loggers needed
to eat as well and the logging continued. Women and some
men needed to save the forests and continued to hug trees.

She tried to lift him up. He could not believe he was so
weak. Everything happened faster. She said: "You must
eat." He looked confused, but let her place a thick water
in the largest pore. "Your mouth," she said, "you are not
a tree and must take the sweetness a different way.

11

I think will call you Rudra, anyway."

Later, she helped him stand. He did, but fell, pulling
his limbs in to keep them from breaking. He looked up
at her, "What can I do that you cannot do? I have no powers
as you expect. I cannot shake the loggers from the earth
like a load of snow. I cannot build a wall of brambles to keep
them out. I cannot even stand and stay."

She urged:
"Can you not tell them what it is to live without need or
greed or narrow-eyed economics. To be within and
not above, to give back after taking, to leave
a place to others ...? Please?"

More people came to the hut to see, while he absorbed
his new dream, not eating, not standing. People
cut fewer trees in each forest. Some were left alone,
and people were proud that they were rich enough to
have forests that were not cut. She told him of the slow
changes. A gentle smile settled on his face. His eyes closed
and he spread his fingers under a beam of light.

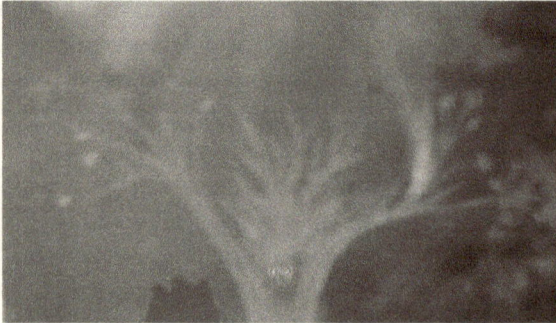

Laurel from the tree (Acrylic on masonite)

2. Taro and Tomoko at Play

Cascading rivulets of everything
excite her flippers and tumble her
body until the cold awakens the
need to surface. Practice songs, songs for
saving the thoughts of those wiser,
farther traveled or more adventurous.
History of thought of crusty old fins in
beautiful sound, hearing them speak in
songs again—entertaining, mating,
giving of sperm and air, expressing the
intricacy of balance and gliding
up to light, creating fluid ideas that
evaporate in spume.
Songs that invent stories to
explain the workings of waves and the
purpose of breathing, the
indeterminacy of water and the
strangeness of air, which we
need to live, and its relation to death, which
we need to live, the substance of
other intelligent beings—the role of
reason to mold the universe and
to increase it. The rhythm of
breathing and play.

The water level changed
so the taste was different, less salty.
Avoiding the deep canyons and the
shadows that play and the
shadows that take, she followed the
stream that lead to prey that
leads now to warmer temperatures
but where food was scarce. The
sounds were strange, but
lead the way to a safe deep.
Pushing faster, faster,
everything was warmer,
but the way was right,
lighter and warmer

13

                         but the way was right
                    A breath and nowhere to go,
                         nowhere everything
                         no way out just
                  lopsided pressure as if the body
                 was deep on one side and shallow
                  on the other. The source of light
                       dried membranes and eyes.
                  Nothing in the songs about this.
                               Nothing at all.

Taro Urashima saw the dolphin. Last spring many came
and were killed. This one and he were alone on
the beach. The killing must stop. He must push
this one back before anyone else came. He touched
its clean and drying skin, how like rubber. Wondered
if he could push without damaging the dolphin.
He couldn't remember what organs were where.
He put his hands under a side, pushing
with his forearms and biceps where the dolphin
cradled. He could not move it. It shifted slightly.
He kept trying; no good. He collapsed by
its side, keeping his little finger against the skin.
He addressed it: "Why do you do this? Why do
you throw yourself to death?" He listened to
his breathing; it slowed as did that of
the other mammal.

                    Another presence, pressure on
                   one side, no pain, just pressure that
                   stopped and a weak breathing beside
                   hers—one of the tailless landers. Pain.
                    She steamed with the heat of change.
              No attempt now to find anything. Rest only. The
                    excruciating shifts—must be death.

Mr. Urashima stood back as the fins extended.
He was dumbfounded. He knew the myths of his
country. He had even expected a messenger someday,
a fox or hare, or badger or cat, perhaps, but these fish
were just meat. Unearthly sounds were coming

from its straining throat. Perhaps he should kill it
out of mercy. Then it became a woman.

She tasted foul odors in her mouth and spat,
amazed that water came out. Her nose was assaulted by
strange sensations totally unlike the sea
Sounds were no longer sharp and defined but
seemed to be coming from everywhere in
jumbled packages. A lander knelt over her.

"You have no hair," he said. "Are you the daughter
of the dragon king of the sea? Are you Benten?" he asked.
Her eyes were slivers, black. He asked, "Are you cold?"
He could see she was and took off his leather coat and
covered her with it. He thought with embarrassment
that he could not take her back with him to Hitachi City.

"Thank you for rescuing me," she said, amazed at the slowness
of sound. "It is my duty to repay you someday."
"Marry me," he said, covering his face with his hand
in embarrassment. She smiled as she pulled and stretched
her arms and legs one at a time. She smiled again.
"What attracts dolphins to men?" he asked, surprised
again at his forwardness.
"Sympathy for your lost innocence,
I suppose," she said spreading her fingers before her face.
"Are you lying?" he wondered.
"No," she protested, "our correspondence, the inner to the outer,
is perfect. We cannot lie."
"Then come with me, there is an Inn nearby,
and we can be warm—" he had become a different
person, unrecognizable to himself, bold.
She sat up, "Are there fish?"
"Yes," he said, realizing that the fish would be
dead and cooked. "I am Taro. What will I can you? Benten?"
"No," she said, "Call me Tomoko," smiling at some
private meaning.

Later, established at the Inn, she slept. He sat thinking
and reliving the day. She had learned to walk rapidly,
although at first she tried to move her feet by whipping

her spine forward. He looked at her—she had kicked off
the sheets. Knowing her origin made her beauty less alien.
He saw her as the source of "yoin." He fell asleep in the chair.

The next day Tomoko said, "Come with me. I want
to go back to the sea for a day."
                              He raised his eyebrows.
"Can you? You can change back?"
                              She looked back at him
without moving—he thought he should teach her how
to shrug. "Can I change?" he asked.
                              "I don't know,
you should try," she suggested.
                              "I have always seen animals
from the other side of the glass of our knowledge, not from playing
with them," he said.
                              "You condescend to us but our world
is older and more complete than yours," she replied; "we have
senses you lost or never had. We are not pets or brothers,
but other beings, other nations caught in the same web
of time and space. And until now, we have never exchanged
ambassadors or respected territories," she replied. He did
not know what to say, so he was quiet.

Returning to the sea, she changed as she swam.
He could not keep up and lolled in the waves.
He saw a gray torpedo streak towards him; he ducked
under water, trying to make sure it was
Tomoko. He grabbed air and dived under, keeping
his arms straight ahead and legs together, whipping
from the waist. He looked at her, the long nose like
a collie's, but with a higher forehead. Flipping
his feet and rolling, he caught her regarding him; after
she rolled, too, he flipped forward and rolled again.
He had forgotten how much he loved swimming. Then,
he had to surface for air. A few yards further ahead,
he saw her roll again and wait for the next trick. She
wants me to do the trick first, he realized. Angling
slightly toward the surface, his movement started
with his neck and rippled along the body to his feet
and pushed against the water with straight toes.

16

He swept his left arm around and performed a barrel
roll, still angling toward the surface. She counterpoised
flippers and barrel-rolled ten feet from him. Then he
kicked full speed for the surface to gasp for breath. She
thought that was good fun and added a tail-slap when
she surfaced. Ah, you can hold your breath longer,
anyway, he reproved her. She squeaked an answer
he did not understand. He took several quiet breaths, then
a deep one, and returned ten feet underwater. He straightened
to a forward glide, arched his back and swam gracefully
in a loop. She repeated it three times as fast. Ah, he thought,
you have big flippers and a tail. After surfacing for a quick
breath, he corkscrewed down as fast as he could. When
he stopped and looked right, watching her effortless
repetition. He laughed, losing most of his air in bubbles,
and had to surface again. He went down. His hands
and feet were pathetically small by comparison, and could
not match her fins and tails. Whatever he did, she
duplicated faster and better. He noticed that she seemed
pale gray, with a pucker mark in back of a dorsal fin. She was
clicking and whistling, now, but nothing was communicated,
except possibly enthusiasm for the game. His surfacing
became more frequent. He realized that he was exhausted.
He began breast stroking toward shore. She leapt about,
following him. He crawled up the rough beach and rested.

She watched him as he napped. He seemed less alien now
that he had been in the water. She could not get comfortable;
one side was always cramped. So, she woke him and pulled
him back into the water. He sighed and went first, kicking
under in a smooth glide. She changed as soon as she entered
the water. He reaching one arm out to try to touch her, as
she came within a foot from him. He thought of a tumble roll
and tried it, holding his shins in his hands. His shadow tried it
but she could not tuck as tightly; it was a good try—her tail was
flexible. Laughing underwater used up the remainder of his
oxygen; he followed the last bubbles up for more air.
She surfaced and began whistling her pleasure. The excited
whistles combined into a scream, then slowed again to a whistle.
He had to surface to talk, since it used too much air, unlike
the sonar clicks. As he dove and swam toward her, she came

towards him, emitting a constant string of clicks. She swam
slightly above him, picking up the reflected sounds through
the bones of her jaw and head. When she was excited by
a new game, her clicks ran together into a high pitched
creaking, as if a rusty locker door were opening.
When she came closer, he stopped and remained motionless.

She tilted her head to follow, then she wagged her head and
dove deeper. She seemed to want him to follow, but he
could not; he saw her shape faintly below him, white undersides
flashing as she turned. As he exhaled and kicked for the surface,
she hurtled past him, her wake pulling him up faster. As they
reached the surface, she peeled off in a different direction.
He gasped for air and lay on the surface, paddling weakly
on his back. He felt her rubbery nose push against his back,
so he rolled over. She came up from below him and carried
him back to the shore. He asked her about the bay where
the waters had turned red with the blood of her relatives.
He knew that the same tragedy had happened the year before.
He was amazed that they would continue to try to feed
peacefully there. He asked her why. She walked away. Maybe
some day he would get an answer.

The next day they returned again.
Shafts of sunlight angled into the depths, reflected
and deflected to exhaustion. He saw air bubbles rising
in a screen from beneath; the air bubbles expanded
as they rose. She kept close to her slow, skinny lander.
He waited until she was close to him, then he extended
his hand, fingers spread. They were ten feet under, facing
each other vertically. She examined it in detail, even turning
on her side. She gave the hand a nudge. He swam closer
and nudged her back. After more nudging,
he held on to her at the base of the fin, and flipped his feet.
She took off immediately, taking him for a submarine
ride; he had to close his eyes immediately from the water,
which was pushing its way into his mouth and ears. He let
go and surfaced for air. She sported around him, perhaps
knowing it could not last, so he watched in appreciation
as she swam. The tail was flat in the water; when it
moved downward, the flukes bent slightly; when she

pushed upward, the flukes locked flat; her whole rear
end moved up and down with tremendous energy. He
thought she might be flirting with him.

The image of a dolphin eating a fish entered his mind.
She was looking at him, making some high-pitched
sounds. He felt strange, wondering if she was communicating
through minds or if he was learning any of her language.
He got used to her blowing bubbles around him; a constant
"pphhuuuhhhh!" He was treading water; she was waggling
her head and rolling on her side nearby. She seemed to
be reading his mind. When he thought of her coming
back to pick up his slow motion, she was there. He felt as if
he were in a field of signals, the water alive with questions
and answers. Play and eat, play and eat. He wondered
if she was interested in anything more. Here was a play
ethic to match any human work ethic—especially his own
in Japan. He couldn't help feeling that both ethics
were overkill; each species could benefit from exposure
to the other. Play in humans was considered
the hallmark of intelligence, indispensable for learning
and creativity. She turned play into a complex courting,
far more sophisticated than anything he had done in school
or at the factory—the factory, a distant memory; he would
be fired no doubt. He took a deep breath and dove down ten feet,
then he flipped his way through the surface and completely
out of the water, grabbing a breath and diving again.
When he came up the second time, the surface was being
churned by a falling dolphin. He laughed with enjoyment.
At first he thought, "haragei."

He received an images of a dolphin leaping far out of water.
The noises he could hear were so complex he wondered if
they sent complete pictures to his brain instead of serial words.
Pictures in the brain; not words, novels, pens, paper,
computers—just pictures in the brain. He received images
of the immense reaches of water; a whole planet Ocean,
spacious beyond experience, his experience. Then he was
overwhelmed with images and questions. How many cubic
miles of ocean? Up room, down room, living room, above
and under room. Did they map it? All of the ocean, or just

where they went? Why did they go where they went? Climate,
instinct, food? What did they think of the increasing numbers
of ships that killed more of their food, sometimes even them?

He felt the weight of a beached companion, the inexorable
falling of a mate back to the water. But in water,
weightlessness; no force, no limits; perfect for movement.
He felt the sea breaking over his beak, streamlining down
the skin and breaking over the tail, leaving a vortex as it
passed. Was he dreaming? Had he changed now?
Freedom of movement. All their art was dance,
imitation and movement. The sea was their buildings,
ships, and clothing. Only food needed effort.
Mating and play were enjoyments. He saw
the metallic surface of the sea from underneath, the blackness
of colder waters, yellow rays probing. They had mountains
and forests and deserts, too. With a leap out of water,
they could see the mountains and clouds of the overworld,
the human thinworld. There were no secrets in their thickworld
of sound. Everything speaks to ears and eyes that collect.
Everything is touch, even sounds.

He shivered and shook himself. This was no
paradise. Men were hunting dolphins. He thought of death,
thinking of images of fishermen killing ones caught in
the bay, caught in nets. He shouted, "You are predators,
killers already. You kill sharks. Men are killing you; do you
know how easy it is to kill men? You must retaliate—hurt
back!" He raged above the water. She swam away.
He wasn't sure what had happened. She returned
and rolled in front of him. He had an image of her catching
fish for food. He had an image of her attacking a shark,
for protection. Then he saw her helping a man in the water.
He understood that she would kill for food or protection, but not
from fear or revenge, and never kill an intelligent being.
In return he formed his own images of the dolphin deaths
at Iki and Hano, in tuna nets in the Pacific, by sportsmen
in Hawaii, who shot them for removing live bait from their hooks.
He formed images of captive dolphins for shows, for research,
for—then she gently mouthed his arm. He was afraid to take it
away, though it didn't hurt. He realized that she was crooning

with her eyes closed. He refused to be put off, surfacing
and slapping the water, forming images of the entire pod
dead. He went limp, exhaled, and sank without moving.
He felt her come below him and nose him to the surface.
She was agitated and cracked her tail on the water surface.
Then she started pushing him toward shore.

He knew from books that, as dolphins developed in the sea,
their brains grew to a larger size than that needed to explain
the simple control of their bodies. That state had been reached
twenty million years ago. The complex brain created a complex
world in a complex and incredibly large ocean. Probably
a world with a longer past and a longer future, with complex
rituals and complex cultures. Aristotle did not know dolphins
well, when he distinguished between man and beast.
Other Greeks regarded dolphins more highly. There was
the myth of Dionysus turning pirates into dolphins to be
reformed from their ways. He read dozens of stories of
dolphins helping humans, keeping them afloat, driving
off sharks. To the dolphin, Plutarch had written, "Nature
has given what the best philosophers seek, friendship
for no advantage;"—simply, dolphins befriended humans.
Humans, on the other hand, did not seem to reciprocate
He let himself be pushed to shore, leaving his preconceptions
sink into darkness. She carried him back to the hotel.

When he woke, she said she could not return again
to the water—she could not turn again. He nodded;
he asked her why he had not stayed a dolphin.
        She smiled, "It's not your turn," pleased with her words.
He started to get angry, "I don't understand. I must—"
        "You do not play enough," she sighed. "You are prisoners
of your hormones, like fish and insects. Nature has taken
only human shapes in the human mind. Every animal
and thing is made human by interpretations. Instead
of stretching your minds, you shrink everything into
a truncated thing to fit inside you; instead of expanding
yourselves to fit inside nature or the sea, you squeeze
pieces inside yourselves." He felt like a man denied.
"I am bored," she said, smiling again. "Things are slow
on land. Let us make some mischief together."

Swimming with dolphins (Acrylic on masonite)

3. Vai-mango and the Fisher

"I am Umusi, named of the yellow bird Oropendola,
and I have permission to try to take one of you
fish to feed my parents." The fisher stood above the river
holding his sharpened spear.

> Coming from her communal house beneath
> the river, she saw a flash of yellow in the air. Thinking
> the light might be from the sun, she came to the surface
> and saw him. Vai-mango moved her fins and rose.

He stayed his throw, knowing this was no ordinary
fish. He reached into his bag for honey
to give her. She swam to the bank and rolled
onto it, changing to be like him. He knelt,
offering her the honey. She received him inside her.

There on the rocks are the imprints of her buttocks.
The nimble sloth who witnessed their union was made
slow for watching. The cursor bird saw the penis
of Umusi and his neck was turned red; the water turtle
saw the vagina of the aracu daughter and was turned dark red.

The Animal Master, Vai-mahse, saw all that and saw that
mankind would continue. He would negotiate with the shaman
for humans to kill a few game animals. The price of
the game animals would be the lives of humans,
whose souls would go into the game animals and not into
the hummingbirds, like the others.

When Vai-mango gave birth to her child, more
animals watched, and they too were changed: The bat
who watched was condemned to night, the centipede
who licked the blood of childbirth was changed to resemble
the umbilical cord. The placenta thrown to the river
became a stingray whose sting produces
the very same pain of birth.

> Afraid now of animals, heritage forgotten, she
> turned to human rituals to protect herself and family,
> rituals of herbs and tobacco. However, when she took
> her son to the river to bathe him, the aracu fish
> recognized his scent and rubbed themselves against
> him, as one of their own kind.

> Later, when she washed manioc in the
> river, the aracu fish would come to visit
> her and she would share some of the manioc
> tubers with them.

Umusi hunted and provided for his family. Peccaries
and deer came to the fields for a share and let
the humans continue to take a share of their flesh.
And, the humans had to give themselves back
as well. Life continued, as it should.

4. Corinen Fades

Rooted in mud, body surrounded by water,
head in air, mistress of three elements,
she sang a motion song:
'My purpose is being
And joy at being seen,
My flesh is summer
And my colors
Are the earth in bloom.
I waste no time
Opening, and the earth
Spins no faster
At my command.'
The song triggered a metamorphosis and her
roots started retracting. Her head and arms
became heavier, her stalk more supple
and she sank beneath the water.

The biologist explained for the recording: "We are by
the Igaripes river, a tributary of the Amazon,
recording *Victoria amazonica*, the largest water-lily
known. It is immense, symmetrical. The large leaves
and flower sprout from a solid stalk, over ten feet long,
rooted in the mud. The leaves are upturned like a tea tray;
their undersides are like a cast iron fabric, ribbed,
ruddy, as just taken from a furnace. The petals are large
and white with pink then a red inner—from one to sixty of them—
they only last a day and a night, then fall apart.
The fruit is olive brown, called water maize." Alan
paused, turning off the recorder, "Can you get a better angle—"

She rose to the surface, as the recording team
watched. Mercedes threw down her camera and
dove into the backwater, gasping at the coolness.
She reached the woman's body and threw her arm
around the chest, recoiled at the clammy skin,
but pulled her to the shore. Alan helped lay her out
and then put his jacket
across her waist, as Mercedes was breathing
into her mouth. She spit out some green slime,

then she felt a delicate pressure against her
chest and she was looking into the deep red
eyes of the woman. They took turns carrying her
back to camp. Lay her on a cot.

"Has she said anything, who she is, what was—"
Mark trailed off.
                    "No, her eyes follow me, and
she seems alert, but—" Mercedes paused.
"But what," the two men chorused.
                                        "Well, her
skin seems awfully wrinkled, more by the hour."
    "It could be just a reaction to being in the water,"
Mark suggested.
                    "No, it's almost like she was
aging by the hour," Alan noticed.
                                Mark frowned
and asked, "Has she said anything?"
    "No, her lips move; but her hands are weak and
she can't hold a cup." Mercedes started crying
quietly. Alan touched her shoulder and looked
over at their mystery woman. Her hair, that they
had thought was light blonde, was now white;
he noticed a fingernail lying on the blanket. He
went to her and gently held her shoulders. She
smiled, her eyes almost black, and said, "Light."
Then her eyes dimmed, the shoulders crumpled
and he stood, throat cramped with sorrow
that could not be contained. He wept as the others
came around the cot.

They buried her husk in the mud.

5. Rinterack Runs

The bar was almost deserted.
                              "Vodka on the rocks,"
he ordered.
              "Not the usual?" asked Rita, unbelieving.
"When do you study? When do you graduate?" he changed
the subject.
              "I was studying before you came. I study in
class, too," she said. He watched her pour. She pried at him,
"What are you studying, Mike Walker?"
                                        "Wolves," he replied
without thinking.
              "Wolves?" she asked, wondering aloud
"Why would a psychologist study wild animals?"
He sipped, then responded, "What makes you think wolves
are wild?"
              "Well," she was surprised, "wild animals aren't
domesticated."
              "What's that mean?" he asked.
                                        "It means
that they can't talk—can't be trusted," she frowned.
    "You mean has no social skills, like dogs?" he led her.
"Yes, I think so, wolves don't interact with humans,"
she struggled with the concept of wildness.
                                        "But you
can't interact with wolves," he guessed.
                              "Why would I want to?"
"And having no wolf social skills, should they not regard you
as a wild animal, dangerous and untrustworthy?" he asked.
    "That's different. We're superior." she asserted.
                                        "Oh," appraised
Walker, "can you smell a storm, catch a mouse, or dig a den
with your hands?"
                    "No, but I have weather satellites, mousetraps,
and shovels." she snapped quickly.
                              "When do you make these
instruments?" he wondered.
                              "Well," she said, "others make them.
I do other things."
              "So, you're more like a termite than a wolf,"

he guessed.

"No!" she protested, "That isn't fair. Humans have a culture, and noninstinctive divisions of labor."

"So do wolves, so do wolves," he said as he walked away, leaving a dollar on the bar. At the door, he turned to her, "Their language transmits information and expresses emotion, just like ours does. See you later."

Rita thought about wolves as she walked home after closing. Perhaps the wolf's clothing that men saw was a hide of their own invention—Legend, nonsense, fears, symbolism, ignorance. The wolf is a carnivore; it eats mice, moose and anything in between. It hunts in packs, families, or alone. It is intelligent. It has a language and a culture. Wolves take easier kills if they can. That is why the weak and sick, old and young, are taken first. Since domestic stock is often dumber and weaker than wild, sometimes it gets eaten. As a predator, wolves are dependent on prey animals. Except in rare circumstances, they kill to survive. She smiled to herself as she walked back to her cabin to study.

He liked to walk railroad tracks. He could go for miles on a rail without stumbling. Tonight he whimpered a bit with happiness. With the joy of motion. He stopped to watch a hare tear off the buds of a green alder; it did not eat them. He kept going, until he smelled deer. Then he turned off the tracks and followed the smell. The deer was numbed by winter ticks. Uncounted numbers had fastened to her and were draining her blood. Whenever she shook, a faint shower of blood stained the snow. Now, she was way behind the others, too tired to catch up. He spotted her. Her peculiar gait gave her away. She stopped. He recognized the tiredness in her stance. She was aware of him. As he approached, their eyes met. He measured her pupils. He decided to test her and charged. She turned and bounded away, but began slowing. He could smell her rank breath, the smell of sickness. He loped gracefully towards her. As an invisible line was crossed, she bounded away, pounding with exertion. He caught her from behind and to the side, with a neck hold, and suffocated her. He worried the neck to make sure she was dead, then started eating from the muscle of the thigh. He ate some of the fatty tissue, some of the lung and heart, liver and kidney. He ignored the stomach and its contents. A raven flew from one fir to another, arcing closer to the kill. She had the luck to spot the wolf before others came. It was just a matter of waiting. She looked for other wolves, before hopping within thirty feet of the kill. She looked at the wolf's expression, accentuated by a set of dark lines marking the ears, eyes, and muzzle. He was almost as dark as she. A movement of the eyes and lips conveyed the intention to eat a raven if she came closer. She waited, listening to the snaps and licks of dining. When he finished eating, she abandoned her pecking at bloody snow and approached the carcass indirectly. He stopped fifty feet away to clean his fur. He watched her eat.

He heard barking a couple of hundred yards away. He answered to notify presence but went back to his place to sleep. The next night, when he heard the series of barks, he made his way towards them. Soon he was running. Then he saw her; smaller, her coat was gray, with rust, black, and white accents. He paused and snapped down at a flea. His own underfur was riddled with black guard hairs. He walked forward, wagging his tail. She was shorter and slighter, probably younger; he was larger and darker brown. They participated in a polite ceremony of nose touching. He was curious and sniffed her flanks, but she nipped him coyly. They hunted together for several hours in the night grass. They each stalked a mouse, approaching cleverly. Each ate his or her own catch. Then they parted before dawn. Her hiding place during the day was at the edge of a meadow, near a stream. His was on the ridge. He felt different. He was changing. He was ecstatic, and ecstasy was needed for change. He had stood out from himself and looked upon a different world.

The next night, they met again, guided by barks and howls. Their hunting world was chiaroscuro, colored only by the smells of blood, feathers, urine, leaves, dirt, sometimes steel and oil. On the third night, they caught and shared a rabbit. A rabbit was easier to catch as a team. And it was easy to communicate the idea; she flushed the rabbit and tired it, driving it toward where he lay waiting in ambush. Then it was theirs. At the end of the sixth night, he did not leave her, but followed her to her hiding place. She turned and looked back at him several times, in warning or invitation; he thought invitation. So when he caught up, she accepted his presence with feminine nonchalance. They slept together and played. They ran and hunted together. Life was more interesting. They were friends. Sometimes they would point their muzzles to the sky and howl an ode to joy, long controlled tremolos in a chorus of two.

The next day, he was hunting alone, running along the ridge. Running pulled memories from the trees, from the soil, memories of others. The vibrations of thousands of pads and bodies, welcoming howls and warning snarls. He leaned forward, his face subtly altering shape, flattening, his legs—the change was so sudden, he stumbled and rolled, gasping with pain. He tried to lie still but the convulsions of muscles caused him to flop crazily. He collapsed. He rested, panting and shaking his head once and a while. He examined his new shape; he had no tail to express rank, no ears to hear; he could still make a face, but it had no connection to truth—the teeth of plant eaters and a mangy look of the sick. He rubbed his forearm, hairless underneath. He knew what he was now, one of the clumsy ones, one of the dangerous pack.

Walking was easier to figure out, but it was slow. He tried running but it was slow. Patience, he thought. He headed toward the territory of what he had become. Soon, in a small valley, he came upon a cabin at the end of a long dirt road. He climbed the porch, noticed a torn blanket that smelled like a dog, curled up and lay down on it, sleeping suddenly.

Rita saw a naked man on her porch; she turned and opened the car door immediately, but before she could get in, he was standing next to her, with a hand on her neck. She screamed, so did he, his voice rising out and above hers. "Hi," he said.

"Oh, shit," she said, noticing the goosebumps on his chest.

"No, no need to. I haven't eaten today."

"What," she started, then realized that he was being literal. "Who are you, literally?"

He replied: "Rinterack I was called, when I was a wolf." Oh, shit, she thought. "I won't eat you or mate

with you; you don't smell right," he informed her.
                                        She stood
frozen for a moment. "Umm, ah I need a drink. I don't
suppose you would just go away or come back
when it's light?" she sighed.
                        "Please," he asked, "I need
your help. I find myself without clothing or things a human
needs to be human."
                        She looked into his eyes; it was enough,
she hoped. She pulled another old blanket from the car
and gave it too him. He wrapped it around his shoulders,
not his waist. She opened the cabin door. He automatically
went first.

She went into the kitchen and poured herself some wine;
She fixed a cup of cocoa for her visitor. When she went
Into the big room, he was curled up on the sofa, his head
and arm hanging over, looking at the carpet. She gave
him the cup and sat down at the counter. She got up
and brought some clothes over from her closet
and handed them to him. He examined them, studied
her form closely and began experimenting.

"If you're a wolf," she asked, "how can you talk?" She took
another sip of wine, wondering if she should get off
the stool before she lost her balance.
                        He stared
into his cocoa, amused with the concept of drinking
muddy water from small artificial puddles—"I think
it comes with the territory, being human." He smiled,
by just moving his lips, as if he were practicing.
She smiled, too, because he was wearing a pair of
her panties, a giant pink shirt, and an old bathrobe.
She noticed the smooth muscles in his thighs.

"I always wondered," she said, collecting his empty
cup, "what do you say when you howl?"
                        He finished
licking his fingers and said, "We tell stories, send weather
reports, express our love, the usual things."
                        "Okay,
tell me a story," she dropped the cup and glass in the sink.

"I was thinking of a short history of my kind:
      I am wolf. I chase deer, who chase grass, who chase
      the sun—grass is light, deer are light, wolf is light
      Across asia, siberia, america, europe I chase deer
      and mice and light. Not alone, no, always
      in a family always at home.
      I was raised by my parents, my aunts,
      uncles, brothers, sisters. I learned
      the cycle of heat, the meaning of clouds,
      the feel of grass, the scent of prey,
      the culture of our ways, how to play,
      and rest, and play.
      I learned to hunt, with my brothers and sisters,
      and with ravens and men, for we all had
      different needs and could share the game.
      I found a mate. We played, shared mice
      and moons and fluids. Our way of mating
      is beyond you—we hold and hold until
      we are dry and fall apart. We made
      a den, then cubs came from us
      and we joyed in their presence
      and the presence of friends who helped
      us raise them, teaching them how to play,
      how to find and eat, rest and play.
      And sleep and play, and play.
      We were many, a populous people
      until you came, other men in greater numbers
      with sharper teeth and faster claws
      to take our food, take out homes. There were
      fewer places, fewer pups, fewer of us. Then none.
      Deer and elk have no one to keep them healthy.
      And light has one less facet.
      I am wolf. I am old and stiff
      I need to piss—our way of pissing is beyond you
      who waste it all to mark a moment's walk
      ah, howl with me one more time for the missing,
      now!"
and he howled.

Rita looked at him, could not understand.
He stopped howling at her uneasiness,
"I think I'll run for congress," he decided.

31

"You humans are a funny sort; you're predators
who've forgotten how to hunt. You act like deer
without limits—just breeding and feeding.
What will you do? Convert all protein to human
protein? Pretend to be bears, eagles, fungus?
You don't know enough." he grinned with teeth.
        She stepped back involuntarily, "Do you
know enough? Could wolves have done better?"
    He was quiet for a moment, fascinated by her
shoestrings, which flopped every time she crossed
her legs. She misunderstood his stare and stood.
"No," he said thoughtfully, "wolves would not try;
wolves prefer to be few; wolves do not breed under
stress. Now, coyotes and humans and rats—they
breed more under stress; they seek stress to breed."
        Too much for one day, she thought; she looked
at him without answering. He was smelling
his fingers, then the air; he looked puzzled
as if his nose had betrayed him.
She said, "Go to sleep, the sofa, I think I know
someone you would like to meet tomorrow,"
thinking of how Mike would react.
She went up to the loft and locked the door,
before realizing that the upper panel was only
cardboard. That night she dreamed.

He lay on the old rough couch, facing the back,
then drew his legs up to his chest, bent his neck,
and slept. He was chasing the deer again,
but he could not catch her; he stopped to lick
the drops of blood. He started to run again
but gave up. She was watching him from
the loft, wondering if she should run away
or if she could afford the cost of staying.

6. Higardin's Time

He lifted up against a Douglas-Fir, his torso lengthening, the claws reaching toward contact. He ripped down through the bark leisurely. He chewed on a chunk of bark as he walked away, satisfied with its sweet taste. He was foraging peacefully. After making sure that the berries had all been stripped from their bushes, he started digging up roots to chew. He was low-slung, thick-set, and very muscular. His legs were short and stout, and strong; the claws on the front feet were longer than the ones on the rear. The outer dark brown fur was frosted with silver. The burly neck supported a heavy head, long with a high forehead and a concave face. An Indicator bird, fearful of bees but in love with honey, flew overhead singing a song directing him to honey. He followed the bird and dug up the nest, eating, oblivious to the stinging bees. As he left, he saw the bird eating part of a comb flung away. He chose a ridge with a view to rest on; a place where he could not be surprised. At night he wasn't as selective, and just flopped down anywhere. He had established his territory already. Although no others of his kind were around, there were cousins. There was an information place toward the house of storms, where one could find news of other bears or enemies. He had visited it once. Coyotes, skunks, and deer had been visitors before him.

Teddy Maitlack sat at the foot of the pine. He had chosen that place because of the 300-foot shooting lane at the base of the slope. He was sure that it was a trail; he had seen paw prints there. He gripped the fore-end of the .30/30 Winchester— his father's gun—and waited. He would add some memories to the gun. He might even get himself a trophy. More, he was providing a public service; he had been told that bears emerged from their winter seclusion hungry and smashed into peoples woodland homes, looking for canned goods or flour. He knew that the landowners breathed easier, knowing that the population of bruins was culled. As a forester, he knew that these same bears killed plenty of good, marketable timber with their teeth and claws. He was protecting the trees, too. The terrain was hilly, with close growing conifers and thick

brush. The floor was mossy and heavily needled. Old snow
covered the north slopes; by April it would be gone. But now
it would be hard to hear an approach. Bears were wary;
their hearing was as good as a deer's, their nose better.
The way they used shadow and cover—just let them appear—
without ever coming.

        The slope was still snowy. He approached, sniffing. Then he
    sat down on his haunches and pulled himself forward with his
    front claws. He started to coast and put his paws on his knees.
        Soon, going too fast already, he reached one paw behind;
    when this didn't slow him down enough, he rolled on his belly,
    scattering ice crystals, and dug in with both paws. After he had
    slowed down, he sat on his haunches again and pushed with
    both paws. This time he got going so fast that he lost
    control and began rolling and tumbling. Almost to the bottom,
    he rolled over a small pine that slowed him. He stopped just
    before the bottom. Sighing with pleasure, he started to climb up.

Two hours earlier, Teddy had loaded the 180-grain hollow
point. He was cold and tired. His camouflage clothing, in green
and brown, was not quite heavy enough. Then he saw the bear.
It was a monster—just what he was after. It was playing!
At first, he couldn't comprehend that—playing. Like a kid,
sledding. Then he realized what he had thought. He raised
the rifle, momentarily unable to find his target in the scope.
He followed it down the lower half of the slope, deciding
to wait until it reached bottom and stopped. He planned
the shot. Then the bear was heading right back up the slope.
He decided to try the shot, although the bear was getting out of
his line. Must've seen him. He held his breath and released
it slowly. Then squeezed the trigger. The report filled every
space in the woods. He was momentarily blinded by the muzzle
blast. Then he saw it galloping back across his line, with that
strange rolling gait.

He followed it at a safe distance. There was still good snow
cover between the trees. He hadn't found any blood, but
that didn't mean that he hadn't hit it. The bear made such
strange turns and jumps that following was not easy. He finally

followed it to a log that had fallen over a stream. 'Blow down,'
he cataloged it. The tracks indicated that the bear had crossed
on the log and jumped into bushes on the other side. Its tracks
looked smeared, as if it was walking funny. It might be wounded
and waiting for him. He had to be careful. Expecting to find
tracks on the other side, he detoured around a hundred
yards. When no tracks were found, he came within ten yards
of the brush. He dug a few small stones out of the ground and
lobbed them into the brush. Nothing happened.

He yelled, trusting that the bear's sensitivity would make him
charge out into his ready gun. Nothing happened. Feeling
a little foolish, he tracked back downstream a ways, then
back up to the log, finding no tracks. He went up to the log and
inspected it carefully. He followed the tracks into the leafless
brush, destroying them as he stalked. A twig snapped.
He fired! The echo was even louder in the trees. He listened;
nothing. He found the end of the tracks. It looked like—the bear
had backtracked! If so, then it went far downstream or
upstream. It must have jumped from the log. He decided
to track upstream to save time. He walked by willows
and tangled pines, not finding any tracks for over a mile.
He crossed to the other side. He was back at the log.
He didn't know where to go next. On a hunch, he went
back upstream on the first side.

This time he noticed a patch of crushed willows
twelve feet from the center of the stream. Tracks led north from
the other side. That damned animal must have jumped
from the stream into the willows. If he hadn't investigated it,
he would have ended up miles downstream. Meanwhile,
he had wasted time on false scents. His anger was mixed
with just a little concern.

He followed the trail back north, towards the slope where he
had first fired on it. The trail was not disguised, now, nor
as circuitous. He had heard from another hunter that a bear
was reluctant to leave his territory, often doubling back two
or three times in five miles. That gave him an advantage.
He smiled. After four miles or so, he lost the tracks on

rock. He wondered subconsciously if the bear had come to
the rocks to lose him. He took off his gloves and rubbed
his hands together for a while; he'd be by a warm fire soon
enough. He put on his gloves and moved back out into
the snow. He began moving east in a large circle. After
140 degrees and another mile, he found tracks leading west.
Another half hour behind. He wished he had a helicopter.
He thought of his father: 'If you wish in one hand'—ahh,
he felt a little better.

The tracks veered once to a spruce with old claw
and tooth marks; that tree was untouched recently, but
a bite had been taken out of one nearby. Edging back west,
the tracks led him to a deer carcass. Apparently killed
by coyotes, it had been partly eaten by the bear—
but not today. He's still running. He must be hours ahead
by now. Several more miles, over a ridge, he found blood on
the snow. So, he was hit. Then he saw the woodchuck hole.
No, stopped for dinner.

He hurried, guessing that the bear was close ahead. He loped
in the tracks. Then he saw the dead-end canyon ahead,
surrounded with scrubby timber. He made sure the tracks
were leading in. He followed carefully, stopping to listen
every couple of yards. Looking around by chance, he saw
the bear come out of the brush a hundred yards behind
him. His heart started pounding—you never knew what it
was going to do—but he forced himself to go slowly, as if
he was not aware of the bear behind him. He concentrated
on the tracks before him. After a nine or ten steps he noticed
that the tracks were slightly broader, indicating that it had back-
tracked him again and circled back. He would look at them later.
When he paused, he noticed out of the corner of his eye that
the bear had paused, also, and was watching from behind
a tree. It was time to turn the tables on it.

As soon as he was out of sight behind a bush, he crouched and
ran toward the rim of the canyon and back toward the entrance.
After a half mile or so, he was confident that he was now several
hundred yards behind the bear. He started to move in, wanting

to catch it before it found his cut-back. He was considering
his shot when he saw the bear's shadow cover his. He turned
immediately, but slipped, firing accidentally. On his seat, he
levered a shell into the chamber, aimed, and fired. The bear
went down. He breathed again, but couldn't stop shivering.

He was lucky that bears were easy to shoot. This one
had evidently figured out the circle gambit and arranged
an ambush of its own. Damn, there was no game
as smart as a bear. This one was too far south, but that
would make his conquest all the better. He wished he had a map
of their chase. He could see blood staining the snow. Bear was
not a difficult animal to kill, if you hit a vital spot—heart, brain,
spine. He advanced within a few feet, thinking 'better not try
to skin it before it's dead.' He prodded its side with the end of
his rifle barrel. The bear jack-knifed up, knocking him backwards.
Tearing the cloth and skin from Teddy's right thigh. By a miracle,
he had held onto the gun. But the bear grabbed his shoulder
in his mouth, shook him, and dropped him. The gun fell. He
caught him up again, face between the tusks, shook again and
dropped again. He clawed him up a third time, by the chest, shook
him and dropped him on his back. He reared back and snorted,
teeth clacking. Teddy gazed up at it, thinking that he could
reach his gun and kill the sonofabitch. He couldn't be badly hurt,
since he didn't feel any pain. But he could see his own blood
flowing down his face, and from his arm, leg, and chest. He was
tired and decided to rest a moment before reaching for his gun.

He hooked a claw into the trigger guard and pulled the
gun over by a tree. He stopped to lick the wound, wondering
if he would die. The hole flowed red. He limped up the hill to a
clump of bushes and fell down. His whole relation to the
earth changed. His gravid muscles became lighter, letting the
thinning bones straighten out. He seemed to give mass to the
air. His muzzle receded. It would be dark soon. The air and
silence were all so clean and wonderful. Tomorrow he—

"Are you all right? What happened? My son is dead. Who
did this?"

One eye open, he froze. Another man stood over

37

him with a gun.

"Can you move?" the man asked. Higardin
shook his head; he felt a binding on his side. "Do you know?"
the man started, then trailed off.

Higardin spoke: "I, I didn't—"
surprised by the strange words, he paused, 'mean to kill him,'
he finished to himself. He placed his hands on his face, certain
that his muzzle had been shot off. No blood or pain, but no
fur, no face.

"I know, it's terrible," Martin's eyes refocused
at a sound like a whimper. "Are you all right?" The wide eyes
might be shock; this man had been shot in the side. Maybe
hunting with Martin, maybe trying to save him. "Come,
we've got to get you to medical whatever. Oh, I'm Martin
Maitlack." He helped the stranger, wrapped in a blanket,
to his truck, thinking, "My son, gone." No scenario came;
who would kill two men, then strip and rob one?
The stranger sitting still, Martin went and dragged Teddy over
to the truck; he didn't remember him being so heavy.
The stranger got out and helped lift his son into the bed.

Martin had reported the murder and arranged the funeral.
He invited the stranger to stay with him until he was better.
And Martin waited patiently to hear what had happened.
"You are reading again," Martin noted.

"Yes, you have a good
library, skewed towards depressing philosophers, but good."
"My father started it. Teddy added that Nietzsche."

Higardin
nodded, "Teddy fought bravely. I am sorry he died."

Martin
paled, "You mean, he, you know, you, fought, you killed—"

"Or he would have killed me. He attacked first, because
I was a bear, or a trophy, or a challenging target." Higardin related
the fight as Martin's eyes locked rigidly on the rifle across
the room on the wall.

"My friends, like Zarathustra's sage in the forest, said stay here,
be a bear among bears, not a puny human. Unlike Zarathustra,
I did not mock them, although I rejected their advice and became

human. There is after all not much difference: we both stand and
talk. We also live, eat, love, raise young, compete with rivals,
go home, share food—we just do not write books about it. We
want to live as much as you do. I will not let you use the gun."
    "Be silent!" Martin roared.
                                        Higardin responded quietly,
"What do you know of silence? You be silent that I may see
you. Speech is so heavy that we are light without it.
Speech isolates you since you cannot feel when you are talking;
silence flows, speech shatters. Listen to me first.
Feel my life first before you judge its value—"
                                                Martin shifted
his feet, empty, sad, lost, still angry, but uncertain, possibly,
grudgingly receptive.

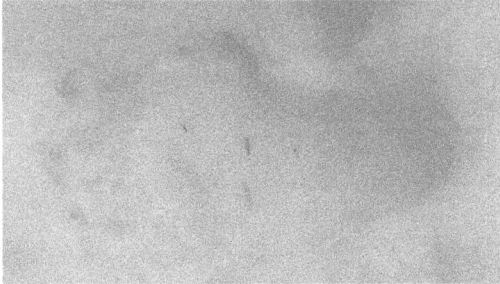

Brown bear track (photograph)

7. The Chance of Anemarea

Gifts from the standing people, gifts of energy
and food. Safe from the blinding and drying
energy. Ancient paths. Breaking complex
foods into simpler foods that can be pulled
in. The center of the cycle of the movement
of flesh, the hinge between the earth and sky.

"Do you really expect it to be that big?" Ellen
asked.

"Yes, I do," replied Professor Beck. "Perhaps
the world's largest living creature. Think about it.
Growing, feeding on rotting organic matter and tree
roots, for fifteen hundred years, 1,500 years, spreading
over 37 acres, weighing 900 tons, and still growing."

"*Armillaria bulbosa*," she nodded; people were unaware
that the mushrooms above ground were just appendages
of the real organism, a tangled mass of string-like tendrils
that spread below the surface. She was also aware that
no one knew how far a given fungus could spread or
how massive it could grow. "How much do we need
to dig?"

"Just enough to get DNA samples for analysis,"
he answered, already mapping out the areas they
would test.

"I can't believe it could be just one individual,"
she shook her head.

"Well," he began pedantically, "what is
an individual? Are you one? Where do you begin and
a virus end? Grass spread from a single seed may be
considered an individual. So might fungi—" She stopped
walking, "What about the pieces of bulbosa that may have
broken off over the centuries? Are these pieces counting
as one individual or many?"

"We'll see," he shrugged.

"Are we going to dig here?" she asked.

"Yes, but use
the techniques we talked about. Try for the edge and
we'll isolate a few cells. Master scavengers, but they
cannot travel very fast—everything comes to them.
Check under that log for the long dark rhizomorphs.
Then we can check the mycelium for luminescence.
I'll walk on and look for basidiocarps." He directed,
then started thinking about the hyphae, fungal filaments
like parts of a spider's web—that was what the word
really meant: web.

A new part of the cycle was beginning, she
could feel the cells aggregating for the change,
proteins making new arrangements from old.
She could feel the growth, soon
she would start—oh—something new.
Things were switching to unknown
states. Stalk cells and something
else. Not spores. She rose
out of the ground

Ellen saw the massive fruiting body appear on
the ground before her; she called for Professor Beck,
but did not take her eyes from the mound. Slowly it
became round, then the round part started rising
from the earth on a stalk, until it was six feet above
the ground, covered in slime. The round part took
on features—human features—two nubs extended
from the stalk and extended towards her. The features
pulled sharp as if being sculpted from the inside.
It was a woman.

Ellen looked at her, white like an albino, small flecks
of duff adhering to the skin. Slim. Cells must still
be differentiating, Ellen thought. She was light,
not more than 100 pounds. Ellen could see the hyphae
still in the soil, running from the sides of the feet.

"I saw," she heard Professor Beck's voice. "Look,
see how the sporangium is aligned to the sun."

Sporangium? Ellen thought, this is a human head.
"What are those water droplets on the skin?" Beck
asked. Ellen placed her finger under one drop;
the skin was cool. She could smell a faint musky
smell. She brought the finger to her lips,
but did not taste the drop.

"Cut her," Beck demanded, "she cannot be complex."
He opened his pocketknife and quickly, before Ellen
could stop him, slashed it through its arm. Nothing
happened for a moment, then small red drops oozed
out the corners of the wound. Ellen pushed him away
with a burning glance, then set about tearing
her sleeve for a bandage.

> I am cut off, she thought, not just by light but
> by this new shape, a small, self-contained body
> with truncated senses, but a marvelous brain
> for entertainment and imagining the things
> that were cut off. How could anyone
> think, though, in the light? Light
> was just for procreation.

"I'm sorry," Beck started, "I had to—" Then trailed off,
looking at the ground. "What chemical substances
could produce this change? Ellen, think of the possibilities,
rejuvenation," he trailed off again, knelt down and ran
his fingers through the duff layer of the soil. "I'll go get
the first aid kit," he said.

Ellen held her up, noticing that the bleeding had stopped,
but that her thighs and calves were still delicately webbed
together. Her mouth was slightly opened and Ellen
could see faint strings between the teeth—like a snail's
teeth, she realized, not differentiated into individual teeth.
"Can you talk?" she asked feeling foolish.
                                              "Nnunnhhh,"
came the reply.

Ellen put her down gently, then turned to get her pack;

when she turned back, the woman was on her side,
running her fingers through the soil, moaning softly.
She knelt and stroked the woman's head.
The woman spoke: "I have nowhere else to go,
the standing peoples on which I depend
are being taken. I have less food,
less territory. I—"

Ellen reassured her, "We have food," wondering who, where,
were the standing ones.
"No," she said. "I have to take
a different form, to move, to get food." Ellen stared
at the woman's teeth, which were now separate and flawless.

Beck returned with a white box. His eyes widened at
the woman, whose body had developed nipples and
light hairs. Ellen acknowledged his presence with a shrug,
but kept looking at the fungus woman. "Do you have
a name?"
"If everyone must have a name, mine is
Anemarea."
"Ellen," as Ellen offered her hand, first
to shake the other's then to help her up; she noticed
that the woman's toes and fingers were curled into
the soil.
"Can we get you anything?" Beck asked,
feeling confused at being out of place.
"Yes," answered
Anemarea immediately, "take me to where the standing
ones go," pointing to the trees.

Beck was driving; they had decided to go the Rogue
Brother's lumber mill. Anemarea stared straight ahead,
intensely concentrating on her mission. Beck wondered
how he would present such a miraculous finding
at next month's conference. Ellen wondered what possessed
the other woman. She looked at the goosebumps on
the white graceful limb beside her, almost like little spores.

8. Re-lill-omtem Tribe

> Danger? No. Danger? No. Danger? No. Danger?
> No. She bent to eat the cold grasses, her
> sisters each taking turns watching
> for any enemies.

He looked out the window of his trailer,
lit up on a moonless night,
and saw a tribe of deer regarding him.
They seemed to challenge him: are you whole,
can you be this complacent naked in the snow?
He stared at them on the edge of the circle
of light, then a frog croaked under the floor
and they were gone.

> She felt a pulling, like being born,
> her muscles twisted until she fell into a
> fetal knot, screaming shrilly. The
> snow suddenly visited its pure
> cold in her. She saw her sisters lying
> in the snow, as miserable as she,
> made naked and vulnerable, hairless
> and hoofless. Then she noticed the
> small light at the end of the field. She
> motioned to her sisters to come,
> but they scattered into the storm.

He heard a pounding on the metal wall;
he got his gun and went outside
around the corner first—a naked girl
was kneeling in the snow beside the trailer.
He smelled a musk of fear; keeping his gun,
he picked her up around the waist and
brought her inside. He lay her on the bed,
her hand flopped and shattered the glass
on the table—he looked at her hand,
with its long hard dirty nails. He piled blankets
on her and went to make soup and coffee.

He placed her hands around the cup and
moved it towards her lips. She drank some
but twisted her head and spit it out on his
shirt. He was about to suggest hot water,
when she looked at him, urgently moving
her lips. "Who are you?" she asked. "My
sisters, are they here?"
He shook his head,
"No one but you was there. I better
look." He left the cup by the bed and
went outside again—the snow was the fine
cold flour of freezing air. He made several
large circles around the trailer before he
found faint indentions in the snow leading
to a grove of pines. He went in, but the tracks
passed through up the hill and over a fence;
he found traces of blood on the fence.
He shrugged, went back, and called
the sheriff; the call went poorly, he didn't
know exactly what to say. He called an
ambulance for the girl.

She was lying on her side, regarding
her fingers. "Who are you?" he asked.
She moved only her large eyes:

> "I am Re-lill of the omtem tribe.
> I always turn lightward before I lie down.
> I lie down out of the wind
> or travel many steps to trees or stand
> together with others, my sisters.
> I chose the best grass, best clover or
> if necessary the most tender shoots or bark.
> We too have a culture, trails older than yours
> and places to eat passed down to the young."

He held her as she stopped talking
and then stopped breathing.

He felt perhaps he knew; perhaps
he could express this by writing:
"There is a way of knowing
That is the way of the deer.

45

You will realize you know it
That you are already like
And unlike the deer
In feeling and thought.

The deer embodies experience;
The vitality and wisdom of
Her body ruins complete rationality
And loosens up our categories—
No monster Pan,
But a small being
Pleased at fitting between the woods
And fields so well.

How can you browse grass or rub
A tree without becoming it? She asks.
Dizzy with eating, exposed,
She scratches the surface
Of wholeness with her hooves,
With her green eyes."

But, the words were light, compared to the body
on his bed. Later that spring, he surprised deer leaving
the field where winter grass suffered the delirium
of weeds. He would never think of them
again the same.

Horsewoman
on the moon
(Collage on
photopaper)

9. The Flight of Parillar

The spot became a crescent. The crescent became a
bird. Fully extended, the wings touched vertically.
As the hand wings, with their stiff outer primary feathers,
drove down, each feather twisted to drive the air behind. The
secondary feathers of the arm wing were kept slightly
tilted to provide lift. The stroke moved the wings down and
forward, stretching in front of the head and body, almost
touching. With the start of the upstroke, the upper hands
rotated the feathers twisted open like blinds, and the
wings were thrown back vertically, tips flexed. They were
drawn backwards and upwards strongly and
extended. until they touched above the back. Then the
stroke moved forward to complete the cycle. The
body was tilted down. The bird moved over the
ridge and toward a tall pine. Several feet away, the
wings were held horizontally. The glide path dipped
below the branch. Then the wings and body were lifted; the
final yards were covered in an upward glide, losing
speed. The tail feathers and alula were spread to slow the
approach further and reduce stalling speed. The landing was
absorbed by strong legs. The wings were folded, and the
bird regarded her nest. She placed another twig in
place on the nest, then rearranged the moss inside.

She dropped from the crown of the tree. She made several
powerful strokes to accelerate her fall; then, with wings
outstretched, she glided in a straight line, dropping through a
gully parallel to the squirrel. She was not seen by the squirrel,
who was eating in a small clump of grass a hundred yards
from its rocks. She came up over the lip of the gully low and
fast. When she spotted the squirrel again, she drove her
wings harder, abandoning the approach glide. The squirrel
ran several steps when it saw her. Then he stopped and
headed back towards her. She was now too high and fast to
hit the squirrel. She fanned her wings and tail, body
vertical and legs hanging down, as if to land. But she
turned and dropped, legs extended ahead, talons aimed at the
back of the retreating squirrel. She folded her wings and

dropped. The squirrel lunged for the rocks as the shadow eclipsed him. She hit him in the rear, her momentum tumbling him several feet, before the claws locked into the fur. She carried him to the same rocks, his eyes saw the haven again. She tore ribbons of flesh with her beak, her wings spread over the warm body.

A rabbit crouched near a hole, twitching his nose. Her head was turned so that a penetrating yellow eye could regard its target. Her interest was keen and unblinking. She turned her head to watch with the other eye. Had the rabbit noticed the intensity with which he was being studied and appraised, he would have bolted back into the hole. Everything in her field was considered by one of those eyes before being marked, or dismissed. Her feathers were dark brown with golden highlights. She took oil on her beak from the base of her tail and rubbed it through her feathers. Each feather required preening regularly to remain straight and functioning. The leg feathers were straight cuffs above the yellow plates of her feet. Each talon was like a sharp finger, precisely manicured, black and polished with a fine patina. She regarded her talons. Noticing a small tuft of white down under the curve of one talon, she caught it in her beak and shook it off. As it was carried in the wind, she followed its movements. She pushed her wings down, jerking the body upwards. As her wings raised, the leading edge was tilted upwards, creating more lift, directed backwards. The hand of each wing was rotated 180 degrees during the upstroke, bending it backwards. The primary feathers spread apart so that air could pass between them, each feather helping to lift. A wind helped her up. She gained altitude. At a reasonable height, she glided downwards for speed, then curved up again. As the air streamed faster over the wings, pressure was reduced on top; the pressure underneath pushed the wings up. She passed the butte, air streaming through the wings with a rustling sound. She dived again, adjusting her long flight feathers. The terminal feathers, which looked like slotted margins, were spread to reduce drag. She wheeled and banked away, soaring over the valley. The flat

planes of the wings were now rigid, like walnut
planks. Her flight was effortless and joyful.

She soared in large circles, searching for the lifting air currents.
She could see the warm air rise from the ground in large bubbles
that men called thermals. She circled higher and higher on the
edges of the bubbles. Up a few thousand feet, the wind
was faster. Her wingspread was large. From the rabbit's hole
on the ground, she appeared as a large, dark bird. The dark
brown body and underfeathers contrasted with the lighter brown
wing and tail quills. Her wings bent slightly at the wrists,
halfway between the tips and her body. The wings were
wide most of their length. The golden leading
edge of each wing showed as she banked to stay by the bubble.
She adjusted the spacing between feathers in response to
turbulence. Occasionally, she twisted her tail to catch wind
currents. Once, falling off the thermal, she positioned the leading
edges of her wings to the left and tilted her tail down and
to the left to slip sideways back to it. To find another thermal,
she flew with the wind, and then turned to face the wind.
She was gliding between thirty and forty miles per hour.
Sometimes she threw a barrel roll or other
aerobatic stunt exuberantly.

Stan was medium height; his bright blue eyes were set in
a confusion of small wrinkles at the corners of his eyes. He
was weathered. "That's two today, ain't it?" Stan confirmed
the count.
      "Yea, slow day," Jim answered in disgust.
"Is she loaded?" Stan gestured to the gun.
                        Jim patted the sawed-off
shotgun and nodded. Both of them ruminated. Jim observed,
"Just ain't as many sheep-thumpers here in dink-land,"
homesick for the Trans-Pecos mountains of Texas. "Used to
get thousands of the chingaladdos."
                        "Hey, one more and
I'll stand ya a glass of calf-slobber when we're earthborn."
Then he remembered getting knee-crawling drunk, yesterday,
not hearing Stan explain how they would come out of
the sun and with the wind to give them two advantages for

the kill. They had seen the black dot on the horizon enlarge to
an eagle. A sheep-thumping eagle was what they were after.

She had been tracking their course as soon as she
had heard the faint buzz and seen the moving dot.
The course and speed were constant. When
the plane angled out of the sun,
she stared straight into the glare,
never leaving the object.

When he was within a couple hundred yards,
Stan lowered the Piper Cub to 1200 feet. Her wings furled,
she plunged into a steep dive. "Let's follow it!" Jim shouted.
Stan opened the throttle and moved the stick forward.
She was pulling away, so Stan opened it all the way. Only
when he went over 120 miles per hour did Stan start to
pull closer. But they had to pull out of the dive to keep
from crashing. She spread her wings and reversed direction
ten feet above an outcropping. She began to climb again in
the opposite direction from the plane. Jim cracked the window
and stuck the shotgun barrel out. They were several hundred
feet higher than the eagle, who was still climbing. As they
dropped parallel, she banked and reversed directions.
She was moving east with strong, regular wingbeats. "Let me
try something," Stan suggested. He turned the plane and started
descending above the eagle, coming down fast in an attempt
to strike her with the undercarriage. She folded her wings again
and dropped. The plane followed, roaring its intention. As
the plane accelerated towards her, she rolled on her back;
the wings now added a downward pull to the pull of the earth.
The talons opened for combat; locked the axle. She arched
and plunged downwards, locked to the plane. Stan fought
for control, unable to see or understand why he hadn't pounded
that dirty bitch out of the air. The plane slew sideways in
a dive, accelerating. Jim pulled his gun in. The scream of
defiance told them it was the eagle, but both of them were
too fascinated by the angle of the plane to search for
the source of the scream. Stan regained control a hundred
feet from the ground. He cursed. "Get gun ready. I'm gonna
cut that bitch from asshole to appetite."

"Ya know," Jim started, "back when snakes used to walk, eagles used to attack planes, throwin' 'emselves at it."
Stan grunted.

> She drove her wings furiously, climbing with sheer power. At eight hundred feet, she folded her wings; the shape of a golden droplet, she dived towards the earth. The angle was too steep. Air buffeted her feathers violently. She felt several pull loose. At five hundred feet she extended her legs, talons open.

Just as Stan was turning the ailerons up, a dark bomb struck the right wing tip. The plane rolled out of control, spiraling towards the rocks. Stan fought to get the nose up. Then they crashed.

> She kept plunging towards the rocks. At the last moment, the wings shot out full. She beat the air before her. Then she struck the ground, quickly drawing in her wings. The shotgun had landed forty yards from the wreck. She stood up slowly, painfully, and let the wind rustle through her feathers.

> The wings could not be moved. She hobbled over to one of broken figures and tore flesh from his side. She tasted it, then dropped the strip of skin. Screamed. She took a run as if to launch herself, then collapsed, screamed again. One wing splayed, the other broken under her, she could not move. One of the feathers cramped tightly, then others, concentrating into dark hairs. Bones became more massive and the beak softened. She focused on a bee on the limb of a pine tree, then the focus softened, all she saw was blue, light blue, darkening, deep blue.

The local newspaper presented facts: Two men and a girl were found near the wreckage of their plane. The girl was never identified.

10. Gan and Ulunia's Patience

> Molten beginning. Temperature, pressure,
> chemical change—deformation. The solidity of time,
> the constancy of space, inertia in the mansions
> of permanence. The slow loss from water;
> the slow gain from water.
> The slow cycles of aging.

"I'm not sure what we can do, captain. These
Pityantatjana people have totemic ties here.
The wind or honeysuckle can lay down spirit
centers with all the associated plants and animals,
who enter them through dreams. If we take
this boulder, we take the dreams, the history,
and the meaning," one of the workers explained.

"We need this boulder for the development near Sydney;
we have gov permission; just do it," Oliver dismissed
the concerns of his workers. The papers were in order,
after all.
        One of the 'Abos,' Ulunia, walked over to him.
"These rocks were the bodies of his victims," he started.
"Those two rocks—The Ulamba man was mortally wounded
in the fight and dragged himself home so that his father
could close his eyes. He did that and died, and in his grief,
his father threw himself over his son. Both turned
into stone, yet carry the seeds of life. You cannot move
either without disturbing our dreams."
                                 "Pretty story,"
Oliver sneered. Grace was running the bucket and it
was just a rock to her—he signaled her to pick it up.

> Temperature and pressure, as if time had reversed,
> or gone forward—no, suddenness was expected,
> traditional even, and given his age, he was ready.

Grace stopped the bucket loader and jumped down,
shouting to the workers. A large man lay in the hole

with his arm over one boulder—the other boulder gone.
"He—it turned into a man," her voice quavered.
Oliver shook his head, "Body must have been hidden
by the boulder. Is he alive?" They all congregated
around a naked middle-aged aboriginal man.

"Is he in shock? He could be schizophrenic or autistic,"
Ulunia asked Doctor Smithers.
                              "No, look, the arm
falls after you lift it. He seems healthy.
All responses are normal; he just isn't moving.
We may have to keep him here for a while."
              Ulunia asked respectfully, "Please contact me when
you can no longer keep him."
                              Smithers looked a skeptic,
but got the name and address of the man who
had brought the patient in.

Ulunia thought of objects and sacred paths; dancing chants,
and clapping sticks. He wondered if the Lightning brothers,
Great Snake, Crow and Crab would call this being brother—
he was now in the bedroom, like a fossil human, although
there was slow breathing. He had been here sixteen years;
the hospital had released him after seven years of failing
to respond to therapy. But, Ulunia knew, time was not
the same rushing stream for a god as it was for humans.

                    All remote now that he was with men. Everyone moved
                          so fast, talked so fast, as if to avoid what could not
                                be avoided. He had to find the proper speed
                          to think and meditate. Take up your walking stick,
                          he told himself. Time to walk and speak with men
                                about the places that owned them. The rate
                                    of his breathing increased.

11. Veronica Nebula

> Extended
> Rising on a base of air

Eleven wearying hours to get to the top of Mount Burton; bad weather,
broken rope, lost glove. But, I was there to challenge myself, to break
through the monotony of school and its mental blocks. I looked down at
a stratus cloud filling the basin between peaks, its top a brilliant white.

> Driven by the turning of light and wind.
> Heart of dust and soul of electrical charge.
> Electron negative charges rising. Condensing.

The cloud came higher, perhaps a banner or a cap was forming as the
boundary layer grew. Small frequent lights, maybe lightning. I wondered if
it meant fog or rain. Ideas, expressions came to me immediately, despite
my physical weariness. A sonnet first, which I titled "Eidolon Lost:"
Much whiter than the starlight on the snow
Your floating form beside me. Lighter flow
Your fluid movements than the dancing reams
Of particles from clouds where moonlights glow
And follow gliding patterns. And clearer seems
Each sparkling eye than any crystal streams
And in them truth that I might find and know
My lady made of dust from stars and dreams.

I wished, an instant, that you would be my lover
Though I knew that you would never love me
As a fleeting form that I could never hold
And I knew that I would rather not discover
That you are as free as the winds above me
And like the careless winds above me—cold.

> Condensing into cells of rolling water and ice
> and into a definite shape, a new shape
> electrical activity intensifying.

54

I put my notebook away and lay back and watched the cloud,
with only moonlight to show it. It was condensing and breaking
up into smaller pieces. One came close. I watched. Layers
and layers wrapped the form until it seemed more solid.
Perhaps it was the light. I could not believe it—a true
eidolon. A woman to lure me to my doom!
She reached down. I stood and offered my hand.

> Suddenly conscious of being born of three parents:
> the earth, sea, and air. Aware of another similar
> form. Definition. Movement. Buoyancy. Attraction.
> A solid water being on the high earth. Tendrils
> of white extended to this being
> who extended a tendril also.

Automatically, our fingers touched. I could feel the small hairs
rise on my arms and legs. She felt—I had held a hummingbird
once—she felt like that, her hand. I leaned backwards, concerned
about the edge. I placed my other hand around her waist
and drew her back with me. She seemed more solid then,
but cool. I looked at her hair and eyes, colored chiaroscuro
by the other clouds and sky.

> This must be the joy of rain, of combining
> and falling, the stepping out of form and unity
> with the particles, I thought. I want to combine,
> so I will extend the two top tendrils
> around the other.

She seemed warmer, and thinking like a physicist,
I realized that the heat could be associated with vapor
deposition on ice—if she was still a cloud. Was she?
"What are you? What shall I call you?" I asked.

She answered: "Veronica," leaving her mouth in a perfect circle
of surprise. How modern I thought, then mentioned to her,
    "It means true image in Latin you know?" sounding pedantically
out of place.
        "I am the daughter of moisture and air," she said
wondrously, "daughter of Shu and Tefnut—do you know them?"

"Egyptian, aren't they," oddly wanting to impress her with
my education, then curious about hers. Her body was refining
its form as she stepped back and looked at herself.

> I looked at my tendrils, wondering when
> they would start to change shape. I looked
> at my whole body; it was different than
> the other's. He followed my eyes, then suddenly
> separated something from his body and covered
> mine with it. We wrapped tendrils again
> but our flesh did not interpenetrate like it should.
> A heavy new feeling, this strange solidity.

We talked. I asked her what her life was like. She answered
vaguely, but then wanted to know what my life was like.
What did I dream? What did I see? How did I live?
How far did I travel? We stayed standing with arms wrapped
around each other (my eyes not reflected in hers).

"Why do you climb mountains?" she asked.
                              "Well," I started,
"because they are there. Many people climb them."
She lifted her eyebrows, not much darker than her white
skin, "Would you climb this one if no one else had or would?"
I answered honestly, "probably not, although I like
to be up high."
                  She smiled: "I understand that. Would you
ask others not to climb some mountains, to let some
be sacred?"
                  I considered the question, but did not think
that my request of others would do any good. I looked
at her, before me, alive, and asked: "Will the mountain
come alive and ask me that question?" She smiled
and seemed to push her toe into a crack in the rock.
I tightened my arms around her carefully and glanced up
with a sigh—there, reflected in the sky, was a mirror
image of us, upside down.

She seemed to be getting colder again, then less substantial.

I stretched my right arm. My coat dropped to the rock.
She seemed to fall away; I tightened my fingers but they passed
through hers. I felt a stronger breeze. She flowed towards
a surrounding cloud. I heard her thoughts, a song
to me or a song to the earth, I was not sure.
  "From your distance I look solid and whole. But change
controls me, I twist and evaporate with the wind. I rise
beyond touch or hearing and move in shapes of fantasy—
although I am bound to the surface by gravity
and though I must touch you to live, it is the rising
and falling that I love."

She wanted to pull me towards her, to fall, but
I knew what she did not know—that clouds,
even eidolons, live only for an hour, less than a raindrop
and far less than a human. There was nothing
I could do. Perhaps she might have lured me
to my death, but by then she was too thin
from evaporation; she had destabilized and broken up
as I watched. Only a few ice particles remained
on the rock where we touched. I knelt and picked one
up; it melted on my finger. Neither science nor art
could understand or express my feeling. Before leaving,
I tried:
        For the loveliest clouds that sail the skies exist
        as shadows on the earth, and I am like a cloud,
        my waking life is just a shadow passing over,
        flowing fast and disappearing when its sun has set,
        then dwells a deeper shade of dark within the night.

I did not know how I would get down. It was as if I was aware
of every possible error and had to plan every movement
and had no confidence that each movement was the right
one. If I survived, I vowed to stay low in life.

Aurora Australis (photograph

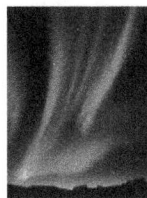

57

12. The Origin of Warm Bodies

Travel, speed, extremes.

At first it was very dark, then quickly light.
Surely the world is ending, thought Mr. Moran,
as he watched the sky pulse blue-white as
the blue-white pulsing star moved to the northeast,
leaving a glowing trail behind it. It fell lower
becoming a yellow fireball. Suddenly it flared
into three pieces, two of them exploding into sprays
of diverging lights. Then bombs detonated
and Mr. Moran was paralyzed by the sounds.
The glow faded and Mr. Moran was left darker
than ever. He had to shuffle with his right foot
touching the edge of the dirt road to find his way
home, toward where the light had gone out.

As he walked he heard a slight hissing noise, then
another. At the third, he stopped and bent down
to the ground. He ran his fingers over the surface
of the road—there was a slight pit, and he felt air.
He started to put his finger in the pit but it got warm
very fast, so he stood up and continued walking.
Then in front of him, he saw a faint red glow,
then another. Must be the parts of the star
and they seemed to be getting bigger. He stumbled
a little, then realized it was a groove in the road; he
saw a faint red dot at the end of it. He marked that part
of the road, so he could return the next day. Not being
a foolish man, he got off the road and found
his way home through the shadowy brush.

He found it easily the next day, a tamale-sized black rock
with a partially melted surface in the groove. He broke
it with a hammer. Just a dense gray rock—no, not one
rock, a lot of little ones fused together. He threw it aside
and kept walking. Meteorites, his wife had said;
he would report it to the sheriff in town.

His fever was wearing off. As he cooled,
he could feel the minerals inside being transformed
into other elements, from melitites and magnetites
to carbonates and carbon compounds. It seemed that,
as the world around him slowed down,
his insides speeded up. The iron inside him
was melting into a red stream that raced
around his body. No acceleration,
no momentum. Had he died? No violent rays, no
one-way pulls, no shattering stresses. Alive.
Had he become this because he needed something
that he could not have in his former shape? Truly
this form had a beauty of its own and his new feelings
had a certain sense of urgency, but the 'why'
was missing. He had never had such senses, broader,
but much slower. It was not like being a god confined
in a small shell, but rather like a small actor
echoing in a rather large temple.

Mr. Moran came upon a naked man lying at the bottom
of a crater, steam coming off his body. "Come up,"
he said, " you could get burned down there." He
started down, but burned his hands on the dirt piled
up at the edges. "Please!" he called down. The stranger
sat up and gracefully climbed the slope, accepting
a hand from the older man. As he breathed, little
black flecks floated away from his face. Mr. Moran
was fascinated and a little anxious. This wasn't normal.

"Are you an astronaut," he asked, looking at the dark skin,
    "Yes, I suppose I am, although it is a long time between stars,"
And he smiled.
            "What happened to the ship?" Mr. Moran
asked, "The capsule?"
                "I suppose I am it, now," he poked
his dark warm skin again.
                    "Was it a meteor?"
                            "No, it was me."
"How can you be here, alive?"

"Energy I think, The energy
was transformed, to this pattern. How do you get energy?
Do you have to take others' energy or put things into
your body and break them down?"

Mr. Moran's eyes
unfocused: "I hadn't thought of it quite like that; yes,
we take energy from plants mostly."

"What are plants?"
"There, that is a plant there."

"How do you put them in?"
Mr. Moran pointed to his mouth, but then had to stop
the stranger from putting the cactus into his mouth,
saying, "No, only some kinds."

"Doesn't that interfere
with the sounds that go back and forth between us?"

"Yes, it could, if you were not careful. How did you change?
Can you change when you want?"

"No, this is new. I am not
sure I understand. These extensions, for instance," he said,
gesturing with his arms and legs.

"Ah, limbs, you used them
to climb the slope, to let me pull you up."

The stranger
touched and released the other's hand. "Thank you. It's good
to slow down, there'sso much to see."

Mr. Moran could only ask, "What happened
to your clothes?"

The wanderer looked at Mr. Moran's outfit,
"I don't believe I've ever had anything like those. What are they for?
May I try some?"

Mr. Moran nodded. He took off his full shirt
and gave it to the stranger, who seemed lighter of skin now.
He kept his vest. Mr. Moran nodded again and spoke: "Come
home with me. I am Mr. Moran," he offered his hand,
which the stranger used to pull himself closer.

"Yes, I see
how useful they are," he said, examining the hand and fingers,
then the tendons in the back of the hand. "Call me Hektor,"
the wanderer said, waiting for Mr. Moran to move.
"What is home?"

          "Well, it is a shelter I suppose,
to protect us from sun and rain."
                              "What is rain?"
"It is water."
                    "What is water?"
                              Mr. Moran had two children,
so he understood how to answer questions, "Water is water;
there is a river of it near us."
                              "But, why would you need
to hide from it?"
                    "Many things are uncomfortable."
     The stranger nodded, and asked, "Do you have time,
time to show me these things, this world?"

Mr. Moran nodded, walked and wondered if this man,
this being, this strange, ignorant, inquisitive consciousness,
had lived somewhere else, far away. Then wondered
how could he bring a naked man home to Maria
and the children? What would she say? What would he do?
A trivial problem. Then, wondered how he could show him
the world. Would he, could he, understand the simplicity
or complexity, the suffering and misery,
or the joy and ecstasy that he would see?

About the Author

Yulalona Leelannee Lopez has a degree in astronomy from Harvard University. To earn a living for the past ten years, her vocation has been investing in commodities; she lives north of Grants Pass, Oregon. Her avocation is saving places and cultures, working through The Nature Conservancy and Cultural Survival. She is an elder of the Tonoho O'odham.

W. H. Auden argued that knowledge of meteorology, botany, geology, and astronomy was necessary before a poet could begin to speak poetically. Lopez goes further, explaining: "Mostly, when I read other poets, I think that they didn't study enough astronomy, didn't get their knees scratched trying to follow earthworms, haven't caught cold watching it snow on their hands, haven't shaped their body to the bole of a tree or crawled along a deer path through thickets—bend or become still or small. I want to speak to these nonhuman experiences." She writes as a passion, to persuade others to her views. Although she has published individual articles and poems in journals, this is her first book.

She is a founding member of the Palouse Poets Collective and a contributor to Rian Ecological Designs.

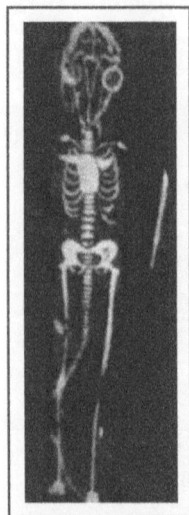

Snake Man (Acrylic on glass)

Colophon

Text Type:	Gill Sans
Display Type:	Gill Sans Light
Graphics:	A. M. Caratheodory
Paintings:	A. M. Caratheodory
Design:	Asia Deer
Publisher:	Calliope Press

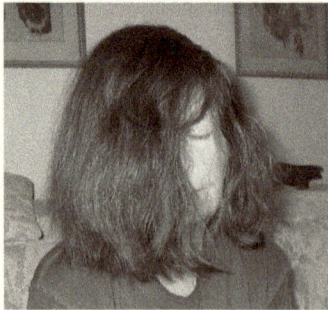

www.ingramcontent.com/pod-product-compliance
Lightning Source LLC
Chambersburg PA
CBHW020951030426
42339CB00004B/55